Collins

Grammar, Punctuation and Vocabulary Progress Tests

Year 2/P3

Author:
Sarah Snashall

Series editor:
Stephanie Austwick

William Collins' dream of knowledge for all began with the publication of his first book in 1819. A self-educated mill worker, he not only enriched millions of lives, but also founded a flourishing publishing house. Today, staying true to this spirit, Collins books are packed with inspiration, innovation and practical expertise. They place you at the centre of a world of possibility and give you exactly what you need to explore it.

Collins. Freedom to teach.

Published by Collins
An imprint of HarperCollins*Publishers*
The News Building
1 London Bridge Street
London SE1 9GF

Browse the complete Collins catalogue at www.collins.co.uk

© HarperCollins*Publishers* Limited 2019

10 9 8 7 6 5 4 3 2 1

ISBN 978-0-00-833362-1

All rights reserved. No part of this publication may be reproduced, stored in a retrieval system, or transmitted in any form by any means, electronic, mechanical, photocopying, recording or otherwise, without the prior written permission of the Publisher or a licence permitting restricted copying in the United Kingdom issued by the Copyright Licensing Agency Ltd., Barnard's Inn, 86 Fetter Lane, London, EC4A 1EN.

British Library Cataloguing in Publication Data. A catalogue record for this publication is available from the British Library.

Author: Sarah Snashall

Series Editor: Stephanie Austwick

Publisher: Katie Sergeant

Product Manager: Sarah Thomas

Content Editor: Holly Woolnough

Copyeditor and proofreader: Tanya Solomons

Reviewers: Rachel Clarke and Jenny Watson

Internal design and typesetting: Hugh Hillyard-Parker

Cover designers: The Big Mountain Design and Ken Vail Graphic Design

Production Controller: Katharine Willard

Contents

How to use this book 4

Year 2 Curriculum map: Yearly overview 6

Year 2/P3 Half Termly Tests
Autumn Half Term 1 7
Autumn Half Term 2 13
Spring Half Term 1 20
Spring Half Term 2 27
Summer Half Term 1 33
Summer Half Term 2 40

Mark schemes
Autumn Half Term 1 47
Autumn Half Term 2 48
Spring Half Term 1 49
Spring Half Term 2 50
Summer Half Term 1 51
Summer Half Term 2 53

Record sheet 55

How to use this book

Introduction

Collins *Grammar, Punctuation and Vocabulary Progress Tests* have been designed to give you a consistent whole-school approach to teaching and assessing grammar, punctuation and vocabulary. Each photocopiable book covers the required vocabulary, grammar and punctuation objectives from the English National Curriculum statutory guidance and vocabulary, grammar and punctuation appendix. For teachers in Scotland, the books can offer guidance and structure that is not provided in the Curriculum for Excellence Experiences and Outcomes or Benchmarks.

Revision of previous years' work is also included, where appropriate, to ensure children are building their skills to become confident and secure users of grammar, punctuation and vocabulary. As standalone tests, independent of any teaching and learning scheme, the Collins *Grammar, Punctuation and Vocabulary Progress Tests* provide a structured way to assess progress in grammar, punctuation and vocabulary, to help you identify areas for development, and to provide evidence towards expectations for each year group.

Building confidence and understanding

At the end of Key Stage 1 and Key Stage 2, children are assessed on their understanding of grammar, punctuation and vocabulary. This is done through teacher assessment of children's writing, through the grammar, punctuation and vocabulary SAT in KS2 and through the optional SAT in KS1. Collins *Grammar, Punctuation and Vocabulary Progress Tests* have been designed to help children recognise grammatical features whilst building familiarity with the format, language and style of the SATs. Through regular use of the Collins *Grammar, Punctuation and Vocabulary Progress Tests* children should develop and practise the necessary skills to complete the national tests confidently and proficiently.

The Collins *Grammar, Punctuation and Vocabulary Progress Tests* are written so that new grammatical content is presented in a variety of ways with increasing challenge over the tests in the book. Previous learning is also addressed in Years 2 – 6 with questions that ask children to recall grammar, punctuation and vocabulary learned in previous year groups.

How to use this book

In this book, you will find six photocopiable half-termly tests, written to replicate the format of the SATs with space for children to write their answers. You will also find a Curriculum Map on page 6 indicating the aspects of the Content Domain covered in each test and across the year group. These have been cross-referenced with the appropriate age-related statements from the National Curriculum. In KS2, each test should take 35 – 45 minutes to complete and in KS1 each test should take approximately 20 minutes. KS1 teachers may prefer to administer each test in two halves of 10 minutes each, and in Year 1 read each question to children.

To help you mark the tests, you will find mark schemes that include the number of marks to be awarded, model answers and a reference to the elements of the Content Domain covered by each question.

Test demand

The tests have been written to ensure smooth progression in children's understanding of grammar, punctuation and vocabulary within the book and across the rest of the books in the series. Each test builds on those before it so that children are guided towards the expectations of the SATs at the end of KS1 and KS2.

Year 2: How to use this book

Year group	Number of marks per test
1	20
2	20
3	30
4	30
5	40
6	50

Performance thresholds

The table below provides guidance for assessing how children perform in the tests. Most children should achieve scores at or above the expected standard with some children working at greater depth and exceeding expectations for their year group. Whilst these threshold bands do not represent standardised scores, as in the end of key stage SATs, they will give an indication of how children are performing against the expected standard for their year group.

Year group	Working towards	Expected standard	Greater depth
1	9 marks or below	10–16 marks	17–20 marks
2	9 marks or below	10–16 marks	17–20 marks
3	14 marks or below	15–25 marks	26–30 marks
4	14 marks or below	15–25 marks	26–30 marks
5	18 marks or below	19–33 marks	34–40 marks
6	23 marks or below	24–42 marks	43–50 marks

Tracking progress

A record sheet is provided to help you illustrate to children the areas in which they have performed well and where they need to develop. A spreadsheet tracker is also provided via **collins.co.uk/assessment/downloads** which enables you to identify whole-class patterns of attainment. This can then be used to inform your next teaching and learning steps.

Editable download

All the files are available in Word and PDF format for you to edit if you wish. Go to **collins.co.uk/assessment/downloads** to find instructions on how to download. The files are password protected and the password clue is included on the website. You will need to use the clue to locate the password in your book. You can use these editable files to help you meet the specific needs of your class, whether that be by increasing or decreasing the challenge, by reducing the number of questions, by providing more space for answers or increasing the size of text as required for specific children.

© HarperCollinsPublishers Ltd 2019

Year 2 Curriculum map: Yearly overview

National Curriculum objective (Year 2)	Content domain	Autumn Test 1	Autumn Test 2	Spring Test 1	Spring Test 2	Summer Test 1	Summer Test 2
WORD							
Formation of nouns using suffixes such as -ness, -er	G6						●
Formation of compound nouns [for example, whiteboard]	G1				●	●	●
Formation of adjectives using suffixes such as ful, -less	G6		●				●
Use of the suffixes -er, -est for comparison in adjectives / adverbs	G6			●		●	●
Use of -ly in Standard English to turn adjectives into adverbs	G1; G6			●	●		●
SENTENCE							
Subordination (using when, if, that, because) and co-ordination (using or, and, but)	G3	●	●	●	●	●	●
Expanded noun phrases for description [the old dog] and for specification [the last race]	G3	●	●	●	●	●	●
Grammatical structure of sentences with different forms – statement, question, exclamation or command	G2	●	●				
TEXT							
Correct choice and consistent use of present tense and past tense throughout writing	G4	●	●	●	●	●	●
Use of the progressive form of verbs in the present tense to mark actions in progress [for example, she is drumming]	G4		●	●	●	●	●
Use of the progressive form of verbs in the past tense to mark actions in progress [for example, he was shouting]	G4			●		●	●
PUNCTUATION							
Capital letters, full stops, question marks and exclamation marks to demarcate sentences	G5			●	●	●	●
Commas to separate items in a list	G5			●	●	●	●
Apostrophes to mark where letters are missing in spelling	G5			●	●	●	●
Apostrophes to mark singular possession in nouns	G5					●	●

Content Domain Key
G1: Grammatical terms / word clauses
G2: Functions of sentences
G3: Combining words, phrases and clauses
G4: Verb tenses and consistency
G5: Punctuation
G6: Vocabulary

| Name: | Year: | Date: |

Autumn Half Term 1

1 Add a **full stop** to this sentence.

That is my house

1 mark

2 Circle the word in this sentence that needs a **capital letter**.

My best friend is called asha.

1 mark

3 Tick the correct word to complete the sentence below.

Don't run ____ you will spill your drink.

✓ Tick **one**.

and ☐

or ☐

but ☐

1 mark

4 Tick the correct word to complete the sentence below.

Yesterday, it ____ all day so we didn't play outside.

✓ Tick **one**.

rains ☐
raining ☐
rained ☐

1 mark

5 Circle the correct sentence.

My granny lives in italy.

My granny lives in Italy.

1 mark

6 Which of these words needs a **capital letter**?

✓ Tick **one**.

saturday ☐
apples ☐
brother ☐
tomorrow ☐

1 mark

7 Circle the word in this sentence that needs a **capital letter**.

Devi likes crisps but i like chocolate.

1 mark

8 Match each sentence to the correct punctuation mark.

Draw **three** lines.

Do you know the answer	•	•	.
The shirt is blue	•	•	!
At last	•	•	?

1 mark

9 What type of word is underlined in the sentence below?

My sister loves to sing. She wants to be a <u>singer</u> when she grows up.

✓ Tick **one**.

a verb ☐
an adverb ☐
a noun ☐

1 mark

10 Circle **two nouns** in the sentence below.

The scared bird hides in the bush.

1 mark

Year 2: Autumn Half Term Test 1

11 Tick the phrase that is spelled correctly.

✓ Tick **one**.

two cups, two dishs ☐

two cupes, two dishes ☐

two cups, two dishes ☐

two cupes, two dishs ☐

1 mark

12 Add <u>ed</u>, <u>er</u> or <u>ing</u> to the end of the word <u>miss</u> to correct the sentence. Write the word.

We walked to school because we <u>miss</u> the bus.

[ ]

1 mark

13 Match each sentence to its sentence type.

Draw **three** lines.

| How lovely! | • | • | question |

| Can you see the butterfly? | • | • | command |

| Take a photo quickly. | • | • | exclamation |

1 mark

14 Circle **one** word in the sentence below that can be replaced with the word but.

Pablo likes football and Mark doesn't.

1 mark

15 What is the sentence below? The end punctuation is covered.

Where have you put your coat ▮

✓ Tick **one**.

a statement ☐

a command ☐

a question ☐

an exclamation ☐

1 mark

16 Match each sentence to its tense.

Draw **two** lines.

| We are going shopping. • | • present tense |

| We went shopping. • | • past tense |

1 mark

17 Which option is punctuated correctly?

✓ Tick **one**.

This is Freya. Can you play with her. ☐

This is Freya? Can you play with her? ☐

This is Freya can you play with her? ☐

This is Freya. Can you play with her? ☐

1 mark

18 Rewrite this sentence by adding <u>ed</u>, <u>er</u> or <u>ing</u> to the end of the word <u>look</u>.

We are <u>look</u> for Wei.

_____

1 mark

19 Write a **question** you might ask a friend at the end of the school day.

_____

_____

2 marks

Total: _____ /20 marks

Autumn Half Term 2

1 Circle the **exclamation mark** below.

Watch out! The pot is hot.

1 mark

2 Match each sentence to the correct punctuation mark.

Draw **four** lines.

Do you like apples	•	•	.
Slice the apple thinly	•	•	!
What a tasty apple	•	•	?
This is an apple pie	•	•	.

1 mark

3 Match each sentence to its sentence type.

Draw **three** lines.

Move your shoes, please. •	• question
How did that happen? •	• exclamation
I've tripped over! •	• command

1 mark

4 What is the sentence below? The end punctuation is covered.

Break the eggs into the bowl

✓ Tick **one**.

a statement ☐

a command ☐

a question ☐

an exclamation ☐

1 mark

5 Circle the **adjective** in the sentence below.

Joe cleaned the kitchen until it was spotless.

1 mark

6 Tick the correct word to complete the sentence below.

Kai kicks the ball and _____ a goal!

✓ Tick **one**.

scored ☐

scoring ☐

scores ☐

1 mark

7 Tick the place where a **full stop** is needed.

✓ Tick **one**.

I sit next to Paula Paula is very funny.
        ↑   ↑   ↑
        ☐   ☐   ☐

1 mark

8 Match each word to its meaning.

Draw **two** lines.

| hopeful | • | • | without hope |

| hopeless | • | • | filled with hope |

1 mark

9 Tick the correct word to complete the sentence below.

Do I have to wear the jumper _____ Auntie Jill knitted for me?

✓ Tick **one**.

when ☐
if ☐
because ☐
that ☐

1 mark

10 Circle **one** word in the sentence below that can be replaced with the word <u>because</u>.

You can go on your computer when you have tidied your room.

1 mark

11 Tick **noun** or **noun phrase** for each option.

	Noun	Noun phrase
box		
the silver box		
tap		
a dripping tap		

1 mark

12 What type of word is underlined in the sentence below?

The flowers made the room look <u>cheerful</u>.

✓ Tick **one**.

a noun ☐

an adjective ☐

an adverb ☐

a verb ☐

1 mark

13 Match each sentence to its tense.

Draw **two** lines.

| Nina hid her sweets. | • | • | present tense |
| Suzy looks for her shoes. | • | • | past tense |

1 mark

14 Change the word <u>play</u> to put the sentence into the **past tense**. Write the word.

Sonya and I <u>play</u> tag at lunchtime.

[   ]

1 mark

15 Circle the **noun phrase** in the sentence below.

Aran watched the green caterpillar crawl slowly towards him.

1 mark

16 Look at these words.

    hopeless hopeful painless painful

What is the name for this sort of word?

✓ Tick **one**.

a noun	☐
an adjective	☐
a verb	☐
an adverb	☐

1 mark

17 Add <u>ful</u> or <u>less</u> to the end of the word <u>thought</u> to correct the sentence. Write the word.

It was very <u>thought</u> of you to carry my bag.

[_____]

1 mark

18 Write an **expanded noun phrase** for the word <u>bike</u>.

_____

1 mark

19 Write a **command** that a teacher might say at the beginning of the school day.

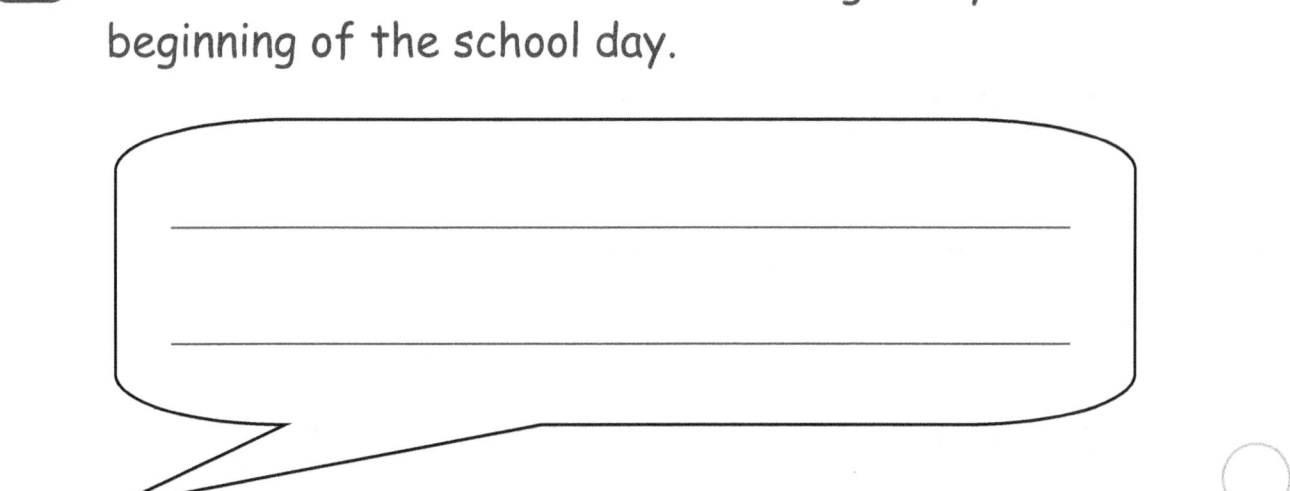

2 marks

Total: _____ /20 marks

Spring Half Term 1

1 Circle the **two** words that need a **capital letter** in the sentence below.

I went shopping in town yesterday with mum and amira.

1 mark

2 Tick the ending needed to complete the word.

	Add ing	Add ed
Stop talk ____!		
Jess has work___ hard.		
Toby has finish___ now.		
Is everyone feel___ okay?		

1 mark

3 Circle the **adjective** in the sentence below.

Alice is the tallest girl in our class.

1 mark

4 What is the sentence below? The end punctuation is covered.

What a lovely surprise ▮

✓ Tick **one**.

a statement ☐

a command ☐

a question ☐

an exclamation ☐

1 mark

5 Which sentence is punctuated correctly?

✓ Tick **one**.

Is Toby coming to York with us. ☐

Is Toby coming to York with us? ☐

Is Toby coming to york with us? ☐

Is Toby coming to york with us. ☐

1 mark

6 Tick the name of the punctuation mark that should complete each option.

	Exclamation mark	Question mark
Watch out		
What is your name		
Help		
How are you feeling		

1 mark

7 Tick the **expanded noun phrase**.

✓ Tick **one**.

the hopping frog ☐

frog ☐

the frog hops ☐

hop like a frog ☐

1 mark

8 Tick the correct word to complete the sentence below.

I don't like spaghetti ____ I ate it anyway.

✓ Tick **one**.

and ☐

or ☐

but ☐

1 mark

9 Tick the correct word to complete the sentence below.

The farmer milked the cow and _____ the chickens.

✓ Tick **one**.

fed ☐

feeding ☐

feeds ☐

1 mark

10 The sentence below should all be in the **past tense**.

Circle **one** word that needs to be changed.

Mum picked up the bags and I pushes the pram.

1 mark

11 Tick the sentence that shows what Mila is doing now.

✓ Tick **one**.

Mila packed her school bag. ☐

Mila quickly brushed her hair. ☐

Mila likes catching the bus. ☐

Mila is waiting for the bus. ☐

1 mark

12 Tick the place where a **question mark** is needed.

✓ Tick **one**.

Can you help I cannot reach my coat.
        ↑   ↑   ↑
        ☐   ☐   ☐

1 mark

13 Match each sentence to its sentence type.

Draw **four** lines.

What a mess we have here!	statement
How did that happen?	exclamation
Tidy it up now.	question
The room is tidy.	command

1 mark

14 Tick the place where a **comma** is needed.

✓ Tick **one**.

Please buy apples bananas and oranges.
                ↑   ↑   ↑
                ☐   ☐   ☐

1 mark

15 Look at the parts of the words in bold.

kind**ness**   pain**less**   thought**ful**   tall**est**

What is the name for this part of the word?

✓ Tick **one**.

a prefix   ☐

a suffix   ☐

an apostrophe   ☐

a phrase   ☐

1 mark

16 Circle **one** word in the sentence below that can be replaced with the word <u>or</u>.

You can go outside and play a game.

1 mark

17 Which **two** endings can be added to the noun <u>harm</u> to make it into two different **adjectives**?

✓ Tick **two**.

ly ☐
est ☐
less ☐
ful ☐

1 mark

18 Write an **expanded noun phrase** for the word <u>hat</u>.

_____

1 mark

19 Write an **exclamation** that a teacher might say at the beginning of the school day.

2 marks

Total: _____ /20 marks

Spring Half Term 2

1 Add the missing punctuation mark to the end of the sentence below.

Do you want strawberry or chocolate ice cream

1 mark

2 Match each sentence to its sentence type.

Draw **four** lines.

Pass me a cake, please. •	• statement
Would you like a cake? •	• exclamation
What a delicious cake! •	• question
I have made some cakes. •	• command

1 mark

3 Circle the **adverb** in the sentence below.

Lily sang the funny song perfectly.

1 mark

4 Write the words <u>do not</u> as one word, using an **apostrophe**.

My cousins <u>do not</u> go to my school.

[   ]

1 mark

5 What is the sentence below? The end punctuation is covered.

What a fantastic day we have had ▮

✓ Tick **one**.

a statement ☐

a command ☐

a question ☐

an exclamation ☐

1 mark

6 Tick the name of the punctuation mark that should complete each sentence.

Sentence	Question mark	Exclamation mark
How wonderful to see you		
Which one do you want		
Can I see		

1 mark

7 Tick the **expanded noun phrase**.

✓ Tick **one**.

the bus was late ☐

the last bus ☐

the bus ☐

catch the bus ☐

1 mark

8 Circle **one** word in the sentence below that can be replaced with the word <u>when</u>.

Let's find out if we are going to the cinema.

1 mark

9 Tick the correct word to complete the sentence below.

We finished our sums _____.

✓ Tick **one**.

easy ☐

easiness ☐

easily ☐

1 mark

10 Circle the **noun phrase** in the sentence below.

Miranda felt shy at the new school.

1 mark

11 Tick the sentence that shows what Mae is doing now.

✓ Tick **one**.

Mae talked to Gran. ☐
Gran invited Mae to stay. ☐
Mae asked Mum if she could. ☐
Mae is walking to Gran's house. ☐

1 mark

12 Tick the **verb** that explains what is happening now.

✓ Tick **one**.

Hani <u>missed</u> the <u>bus</u> and <u>is walking</u> home.
       ☐   ☐   ☐

1 mark

13 The sentence below should all be in the **past tense**.

Circle **one** word that needs to be changed.

We jumped over the puddles and splash in the stream.

1 mark

14 Tick the correct word to complete the sentence below.

We ran ____ to the sea.

✓ Tick **one**.

happily ☐

happy ☐

happiness ☐

1 mark

15 Tick the correct word to complete the sentence below.

I'm sorry but we cannot come today ____ Pavel has hurt his foot.

✓ Tick **one**.

and ☐

if ☐

because ☐

that ☐

1 mark

16 Write the words that tell you that this is happening <u>now</u>.

Mum is talking to the lady next door.

_____

1 mark

17 Tick the place where a **comma** is needed.

✓ Tick **one**.

Liam invited Max Sunil and Ben to his party.
              ↑   ↑   ↑
              □   □   □

1 mark

18 Are these sentences in the **present tense** or the **past tense**? Tick one box in each row.

Sentence	Present tense	Past tense
The fox hunts at night.		
The rabbit was scared.		
The owl is looking for mice.		
The bat slept upside down.		

1 mark

19 Write a **question** that you might be asked at lunchtime.

_____

_____

2 marks

Total: _____ /20 marks

Summer Half Term 1

1 Which option is punctuated correctly?

✓ Tick **one**.

The swimming gala is on saturday. ☐

The swimming gala is on Saturday. ☐

The swimming gala is on Saturday? ☐

The swimming gala is on saturday? ☐

1 mark

2 Match the words to make **compound nouns**.

Draw **four** lines.

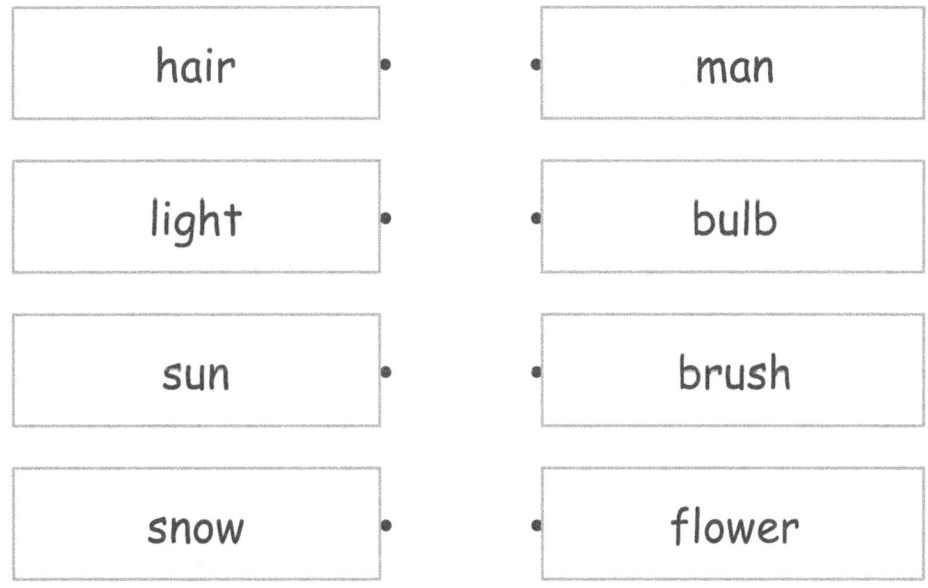

1 mark

3 Tick the place where a **comma** is needed.

✓ Tick **one**.

Daisy loves singing ☐ dancing ☐ and ☐ playing football.

1 mark

4 Circle the correct word.

Let / Let's bake a cake.

1 mark

5 Tick the name of the punctuation mark that should go at the end of each option.

Sentence	Question mark	Full stop
What shall we do		
We need to go shopping		
Put it on the table, please		

1 mark

6 The end punctuation is missing from the sentences below. Which sentence is a **command**?

✓ Tick **one**.

I would like some chocolate ☐

Can I have a piece of chocolate ☐

What a lot of chocolate ☐

Give me a piece of chocolate ☐

1 mark

7 Tick the correct word to complete the sentence below.

We went to _____ house after school.

✓ Tick **one**.

Sophie ☐

Sophies ☐

Sophie's ☐

1 mark

8 Circle the correct word.

That boy is Jamal's / Jamals brother.

1 mark

9 Tick the correct word to complete the sentence below.

The bell rang _____ at the end of break.

✓ Tick **one**.

loud ☐

loudly ☐

loudness ☐

1 mark

10 Write the words <u>has not</u> as one word, using an **apostrophe**.

The shirt I ordered <u>has not</u> arrived.

[   ]

1 mark

11 Are these sentences in the **present tense** or the **past tense**? Tick one box in each row.

Sentence	Present tense	Past tense
It snowed last night.		
We made a snowman.		
It has a carrot for its nose.		
The snowman looks like Dad.		

1 mark

12 Tick the correct word to complete the sentence below.

Usha ran the ____ and won the race.

✓ Tick **one**.

fast ☐
faster ☐
fastest ☐

1 mark

13 The sentence below should all be in the **present tense**.

Circle **one** word that needs to be changed.

Billy goes to Kit's house when his dad worked late.

1 mark

14 Choose **one** of these words to complete the **compound noun** in the sentence below.

stead   sit   room

Please tidy your bed_____ before we leave.

1 mark

15 Are these sentences in the **present tense** or the **past tense**? Tick **one** box in each row.

Sentence	Present tense	Past tense
We are running fast.		
They were running slowly.		
Kamla was jumping high.		
I am running on the spot.		

1 mark

16 Tick the sentence that tells you what is happening <u>now</u>.

✓ Tick **one**.

Sam was playing football. ☐
Nik is watching television. ☐
Asif likes karate. ☐
Mia danced all day. ☐

1 mark

17 Explain how you know that the sentence below is in the **past tense**.

We walked back from school slowly.

_____

1 mark

18 Rewrite the sentence below correctly as **two** sentences. Add in the missing punctuation.

Is there anything to eat I'm hungry

_____

_____

1 mark

19 Write a **command** that a parent might give a child during breakfast.

_____

_____

2 marks

Total: _____ /20 marks

Year 2: Summer Half Term Test 2

Name: Year: Date:

Summer Half Term 2

1 Circle **one** word that needs a capital letter in the sentence below.

Tomorrow i am going to Ava's party.

1 mark

2 Which option is punctuated correctly?

✓ Tick **one**.

Jaz and millie play hockey in tamworth. ☐

Jaz and Millie play Hockey in Tamworth. ☐

Jaz and Millie play Hockey in tamworth. ☐

Jaz and Millie play hockey in Tamworth. ☐

1 mark

3 Match the words to make compound words.

Draw **four** lines.

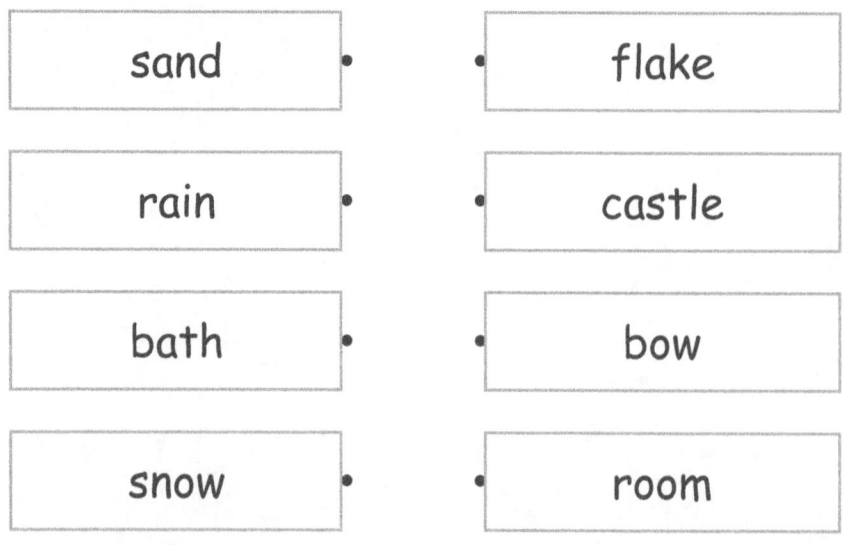

1 mark

4 What is the sentence below? The end punctuation is covered.

Naveen wants to watch the television

✓ Tick **one**.

a statement ☐

a command ☐

a question ☐

an exclamation ☐

1 mark

5 Write the missing word ending to complete each sentence.

Sentence	Missing ending
Why are you cry___?	
Stop fight___!	
We have all calm___ down.	
They play___ for ages.	

1 mark

6 Explain why the word <u>Wednesday</u> has a **capital letter** in the sentence below.

The parcel will arrive on Wednesday.

_____

1 mark

7 Which option is punctuated correctly?

✓ Tick **one**.

What is that boys name? ☐

What is that boys' name? ☐

What is that boy's name? ☐

1 mark

8 Write the words <u>could not</u> as one word, using an **apostrophe**.

My mum <u>could not</u> come on the trip with us.

[   ]

1 mark

9 Tick the correct option to complete the sentence below.

I am good at Maths _____ I find spelling hard.

✓ Tick **one**.

but	☐
if	☐
or	☐
that	☐

1 mark

10 Circle one word in the sentence below that can be replaced with the word <u>because</u>.

I did not want to go to school when I had a stomach ache.

1 mark

11 Tick the **noun phrase** below.

✓ Tick **one**.

the fog was thick	☐
fog	☐
a foggy day	☐
I hate fog	☐

1 mark

12 Decide whether each word is a **noun**, an **adjective**, a **verb** or an **adverb**. Tick **one** box in each row.

Word	Noun	Adjective	Verb	Adverb
build				
builder				
hard				
quickly				

1 mark

13 Tick the place where a **comma** is needed.

✓ Tick **one**.

Put away the pens pencils and paper quickly.

1 mark

14 Tick the correct word to complete the sentence below.

An elephant is ____ than a horse.

✓ Tick **one**.

strong ☐

stronger ☐

strongest ☐

1 mark

15 **Circle** the **adverb** in the sentence below.

Molly's new shoes squeaked loudly.

1 mark

16 Circle the **noun phrase** in the sentence below.

Can I have the next turn?

1 mark

17 Which **two** endings can be added to the noun pain to make it into two different **adjectives**?

✓ Tick **two**.

ful ☐

ed ☐

less ☐

ing ☐

1 mark

18 Tick **two** sentences that include an action in progress.

✓ Tick **two**.

We were carrying the tray carefully. ☐

We carried the tray carefully. ☐

Meg is cleaning the board. ☐

Meg cleans the board. ☐

1 mark

19 The sentence below is in the **present tense**. Rewrite the sentence in the **past tense**.

Tina cooks the dinner then cleans the kitchen.

_____

_____

1 mark

20 Rewrite the sentence below correctly as **two** sentences. Add in the missing punctuation.

Shall we go out I think the rain has stopped

_____

_____

1 mark

Total: _____ /20 marks

Mark scheme for Autumn Half Term 1

Qu.	Requirement	Mark
1 G5	**Award 1 mark** for the full stop added.	1m
2 G5	**Award 1 mark** for the name *asha* circled. **Also award the mark** for the letter *a* circled or the name *Asha* written with a capital letter.	1m
3 G3	**Award 1 mark** for a tick in the box next to *or*. **Also award the mark** for the word *or* circled or written in to complete the sentence.	1m
4 G6	**Award 1 mark** for a tick in the box next to *rained*. **Also award the mark** for the word *rained* circled or written in to complete the sentence.	1m
5 G5	**Award 1 mark** for the sentence *My granny lives in Italy.* circled.	1m
6 G5	**Award 1 mark** for a tick in the box next to *saturday*. **Also award the mark** for the word *Saturday* written correctly.	1m
7 G5	**Award 1 mark** for the word *i* circled. **Also award the mark** for the word *I* written correctly.	1m
8 G5	**Award 1 mark** for all three lines drawn correctly: Do you know the answer = ? The shirt is blue = . At last = !	1m
9 G1	**Award 1 mark** for a tick in the box next to *a noun*. **Also award the mark** for the word *a noun* circled.	1m
10 G1	**Award 1 mark** for the words *bird* and *bush* circled.	1m
11 G6	**Award 1 mark** for a tick in the box next to *two cups, two dishes*. **Also award the mark** for the words *two cups, two dishes* circled.	1m
12 G6	**Award 1 mark** for the word *missed* written correctly in the box.	1m
13 G2	**Award 1 mark** for all three lines drawn correctly: How lovely! = exclamation Can you see the butterfly? = question Take a photo quickly. = command	1m
14 G3	**Award 1 mark** for the word *and* circled.	1m
15 G2	**Award 1 mark** for a tick in the box next to *a question*.	1m
16 G4	**Award 1 mark** for both lines drawn correctly: We are going shopping. = present tense We went shopping. = past tense	1m
17 G5	**Award 1 mark** for a tick in the box next to *This is Freya. Can you play with her?*	1m
18 G6	**Award 1 mark** for the sentence *We are looking for Wei.* written correctly.	1m
19 G2	**Award 1 mark** for a sentence that matches the brief with spaces between the words. **Award 1 mark** for a capital letter and a question mark used correctly. (Total 2 marks)	2m

Year 2: Autumn Half Term Test 2 – Mark scheme

Mark scheme for Autumn Half Term 2

Qu.	Requirement	Mark
1 G5	**Award 1 mark** for the exclamation mark circled.	1m
2 G5	**Award 1 mark** for all four lines drawn correctly: Do you like apples = ? Slice the apple thinly = . What a tasty apple = ! This is an apple pie = .	1m
3 G2	**Award 1 mark** for all three lines drawn correctly: Move your shoes, please. = command How did that happen? = question I've tripped over! = exclamation	1m
4 G2	**Award 1 mark** for a tick in the box next to *a command*.	1m
5 G1	**Award 1 mark** for the word *spotless* circled.	1m
6 G4	**Award 1 mark** for a tick in the box next to *scores*.	1m
7 G5	**Award 1 mark** for a tick in the box under the space between *Paula* and *Paula*.	1m
8 G6	**Award 1 mark** for both lines drawn correctly: hopeful = filled with hope hopeless = without hope	1m
9 G3	**Award 1 mark** for a tick in the box next to *that*.	1m
10 G3	**Award 1 mark** for the word *when* circled.	1m
11 G3	**Award 1 mark** for three or four correct answers: box = Noun the silver box = Noun phrase tap = Noun a dripping tap = Noun phrase	1m
12 G6	**Award 1 mark** for a tick in the box next to *an adjective*.	1m
13 G4	**Award 1 mark** for both lines drawn correctly: Nina hid her sweets. = past tense Suzy looks for her shoes. = present tense	1m
14 G4	**Award 1 mark** for the word *played* written in the box.	1m
15 G3	**Award 1 mark** for the phrase *the green caterpillar* circled. Do not award a mark for *green caterpillar* or *caterpillar* or *green caterpillar crawl* circled.	1m
16 G1 G6	**Award 1 mark** for a tick in the box next to *an adjective*.	1m
17 G6	**Award 1 mark** for the word *thoughtful* written in the box.	1m
18 G3	**Award 1 mark** for a suitable noun phrase written correctly, for example: *this bike, my new bike, Paul's old bike, that bike over there*.	1m
19 G2	**Award 1 mark** for a command that matches the brief with spaces between the words. **Award 1 mark** for a capital letter and a full stop used correctly. (Total 2 marks)	2m

Mark scheme for Spring Half Term 1

Qu.	Requirement	Mark
1 G5	**Award 1 mark** for the words *mum* and *amira* circled.	1m
2 G6	**Award 1 mark** for three or four correct answers: Stop talk____ = Add ing Jess has work____ hard.= Add ed Toby has finish_____ now. = Add ed Is everyone feel____ okay? = Add ing	1m
3 G1	**Award 1 mark** for the word *tallest* circled.	1m
4 G2	**Award 1 mark** for a tick in the box next to *an exclamation*.	1m
5 G5	**Award 1 mark** for a tick in the box next to *Is Toby coming to York with us?*	1m
6 G5	**Award 1 mark** for three or four correct answers: Watch out = Exclamation mark What is your name = Question mark Help = Exclamation mark How are you feeling = Question mark	1m
7 G3	**Award 1 mark** for a tick in the box next to *the hopping frog*.	1m
8 G3	**Award 1 mark** for a tick in the box next to *but*.	1m
9 G4	**Award 1 mark** for a tick in the box next to *fed*.	1m
10 G4	**Award 1 mark** for the word *pushes* circled.	1m
11 G4	**Award 1 mark** for a tick in the box next to *Mila is waiting for the bus*.	1m
12 G5	**Award 1 mark** for a tick in the box under the space between *help* and *I*.	1m
13 G2	**Award 1 mark** for all four lines drawn correctly: What a mess we have here! = exclamation How did that happen? = question Tidy it up now. = command The room is tidy. = statement	1m
14 G5	**Award 1 mark** for a tick in the box under the space between *apples* and *bananas*.	1m
15 G6	**Award 1 mark** for a tick in the box next to *a suffix*.	1m
16 G3	**Award 1 mark** for the word *and* circled.	1m
17 G6	**Award 1 mark** for ticks in the boxes next to *less and ful*.	1m
18 G3	**Award 1 mark** for a suitable noun phrase written correctly, for example: *his woolly hat, my hat, the hat with a bobble, this hat*.	1m
19 G2	**Award 1 mark** for an exclamation that matches the brief with spaces between the words. **Award 1 mark** for a capital letter and an exclamation mark used correctly. (Total 2 marks)	2m

Year 2: Spring Half Term Test 2 – Mark scheme

Mark scheme for Spring Half Term 2

Qu.	Requirement	Mark
1 G2 G5	**Award 1 mark** for a question mark added to the end of the sentence.	1m
2 G2	**Award 1 mark** for all four lines drawn correctly: Pass me a cake, please. = command Would you like a cake? = question What a delicious cake! = exclamation I have made some cakes. = statement	1m
3 G1	**Award 1 mark** for the word *perfectly* circled.	1m
4 G5	**Award 1 mark** for the word *don't* written in the box correctly.	1m
5 G2	**Award 1 mark** for a tick in the box next to *an exclamation*.	1m
6 G2 G5	**Award 1 mark** for all three answers correct: How wonderful to see you = Exclamation mark Which one do you want = Question mark Can I see = Question mark	1m
7 G3	**Award 1 mark** for a tick in the box next to *the last bus*.	1m
8 G3	**Award 1 mark** for the word *if* circled.	1m
9 G6	**Award 1 mark** for a tick in the box next to *easily*.	1m
10 G3	**Award 1 mark** for the phrase *the new school* circled.	1m
11 G4	**Award 1 mark** for a tick in the box next to *Mae is walking to Gran's house*.	1m
12 G4	**Award 1 mark** for a tick in the box under *is walking*.	1m
13 G4	**Award 1 mark** for the word *splash* circled.	1m
14 G6	**Award 1 mark** for a tick in the box next to *happily*.	1m
15 G3	**Award 1 mark** for a tick in the box next to *because*.	1m
16 G4	**Award 1 mark** for the words *is talking* written on the line.	1m
17 G5	**Award 1 mark** for a tick in the box under the space between *Max* and *Sunil*.	1m
18 G4	**Award 1 mark** for three or four correct answers: The fox hunts at night. = Present tense The rabbit was scared. = Past tense The owl is looking for mice. = Present tense The bat slept upside down. = Past tense	1m
19 G2	**Award 1 mark** for a question that matches the brief with spaces between the words. **Award 1 mark** for a capital letter and a question mark used correctly. (Total 2 marks)	2m

Mark scheme for Summer Half Term 1

Qu.	Requirement	Mark
1 G5	**Award 1 mark** for a tick in the box next to *The swimming gala is on Saturday.*	1m
2 G1	**Award 1 mark** for all four lines drawn correctly: hair = brush light = bulb sun = flower snow = man	1m
3 G5	**Award 1 mark** for a tick in the box under the space between *singing* and *dancing*.	1m
4 G5	**Award 1 mark** for the word *Let's* circled.	1m
5 G5	**Award 1 mark** for all three answers correct: What shall we do = Question mark We need to go shopping = Full stop Put it on the table, please = Full stop	1m
6 G2	**Award 1 mark** for a tick in the box next to *Give me a piece of chocolate.*	1m
7 G5	**Award 1 mark** for a tick in the box next to *Sophie's.*	1m
8 G5	**Award 1 mark** for the word *Jamal's* circled.	1m
9 G1 G6	**Award 1 mark** for a tick in the box next to *loudly*.	1m
10 G5	**Award 1 mark** for the word *hasn't* written in the box.	1m
11 G4	**Award 1 mark** for four correct answers: It snowed last night. = Past tense We made a snowman. = Past tense It has a carrot for its nose. = Present tense The snowman looks like Dad. = Present tense	1m
12 G6	**Award 1 mark** for a tick in the box next to *fastest*.	1m
13 G4	**Award 1 mark** for the word *worked* circled.	1m
14 G1 G6	**Award 1 mark** for the word *room* written on the line.	1m
15 G4	**Award 1 mark** for four correct answers: We are running fast. = Present tense They were running slowly. = Past tense Kamla was jumping high. = Past tense I am running on the spot. = Present tense	1m
16 G4	**Award 1 mark** for a tick in the box next to *Nik is watching television.*	1m

Year 2: Summer Half Term Test 1 – Mark scheme

Qu.	Requirement	Mark
17 G4	**Award 1 mark** for a suitable explanation, for example: *The verb walked has the letters ed at the end and this means it is in the past tense.*	1m
18 G2	**Award 1 mark** for the sentences: *Is there anything to eat? I'm hungry!* or *Is there anything to eat? I'm hungry.*	1m
19 G2	**Award 1 mark** for a command that matches the brief with spaces between the words. **Award 1 mark** for a capital letter and a full stop used correctly. (Total 2 marks)	2m

Mark scheme for Summer Half Term 2

Qu.	Requirement	Mark
1 G5	**Award 1 mark** for the word *i* circled.	1m
2 G5	**Award 1 mark** for a tick in the box next to *Jaz and Millie play hockey in Tamworth.*	1m
3 G1 G6	**Award 1 mark** for all four lines drawn correctly: sand = castle rain = bow bath = room snow = flake	1m
4 G2	**Award 1 mark** for a tick in the box next to *a statement.*	1m
5 G6	**Award 1 mark** for all four answers correct. Why are you cry____? = ing Stop fight____! = ing We have all calm____ down. = ed They play____ for ages. = ed	1m
6 G5	**Award 1 mark** for a suitable answer, for example: *Wednesday has a capital letter because it is a day of the week.* Do not award a mark for *because it is a name.*	1m
7 G5	**Award 1 mark** for a tick in the box next to *What is that boy's name?*	1m
8 G5	**Award 1 mark** for the word *couldn't* written correctly in the box.	1m
9 G3	**Award 1 mark** for a tick in the box next to *but.*	1m
10 G3	**Award 1 mark** for the word *when* circled.	1m
11 G3	**Award 1 mark** for a tick in the box next to *a foggy day.*	1m
12 G1	**Award 1 mark** for all four answers correct: build = Verb builder = Noun hard = Adjective quickly = Adverb	1m
13 G5	**Award 1 mark** for a tick in the box under the space between *pens* and *pencils.*	1m
14 G1 G6	**Award 1 mark** for a tick in the box next to *stronger.*	1m
15 G1	**Award 1 mark** for the word *loudly* circled.	1m
16 G3	**Award 1 mark** for the phrase *the next turn* circled.	1m
17 G6	**Award 1 mark** for ticks in the boxes next to *ful* and *less.* Do not award a mark for a tick in the box next to *ed* (it is a verb).	1m

Year 2: Summer Half Term Test 2 – Mark scheme

Qu.	Requirement	Mark
18 G4	**Award 1 mark** for ticks in the boxes next to *We were carrying the tray carefully.* and *Meg is cleaning the board.* Do not award the mark if more than two boxes are ticked.	1m
19 G4	**Award 1 mark** for *Tina cooked the dinner then cleaned the kitchen.* Do not award a mark if only one of the two verbs is correct.	1m
20 G2	**Award 1 mark** for the two sentences *Shall we go out? I think the rain has stopped.* Do not award a mark if only one of the punctuation marks is correct.	1m

Name: Class:

Year 2 Grammar, Punctuation and Vocabulary Record Sheet

Tests	Mark	Total marks	Key skills to target
Autumn Half Term Test 1			
Autumn Half Term Test 2			
Spring Half Term Test 1			
Spring Half Term Test 2			
Summer Half Term Test 1			
Summer Half Term Test 2			

www.ingramcontent.com/pod-product-compliance
Lightning Source LLC
Chambersburg PA
CBHW081419300426
44109CB00019BA/2353